ESSENTIAL TIPS

Making

SALADS

D0061466

ESSENTIAL  TIPS

Making

SALADS

Anne Willan

DORLING KINDERSLEY

London • New York • Stuttgart • Moscow

A Dorling Kindersley Book

Editor Simon Adams
Art Editor Alison Shackleton
Series Editor Charlotte Davies
Series Art Editor Clive Hayball
Production Controller Lauren Britton

First published in Great Britain in 1996 by
Dorling Kindersley Limited,
9 Henrietta Street, London WC2E 8PS
Reprinted 1996, 1997

A CIP catalogue record for this book is available from the British Library

ISBN 0-7513-0277-5

Text film output by The Right Type, Great Britain
Reproduced by Colourscan, Singapore
Printed and bound by Graphicom, Italy

Author's note: Salt and pepper can be added to most recipes.
Season according to your own taste.

ESSENTIAL TIPS

PAGES 68–69

SALAD
KNOW-HOW

WHICH SALAD?

1 SALADS FOR HEALTH

A well-chosen salad, with a balance of ingredients united by an appropriate dressing, is the healthiest of meals. If you are concerned about your calorie intake, prepare salads with little added fat and plenty of protein.

◁ **LETTUCE**
Lettuces do not contain fat or cholesterol, and are low in carbohydrates. Many contain little or no sodium.

△ **TOMATO**
Tomatoes contain no fat or cholesterol and are low in sodium and carbohydrates.

Celery has a high sodium content

CELERY ▷
Celery contains no cholesterol or fat, and is low in carbohydrates.

HIGH-CALORIE INGREDIENTS
If you are watching your weight, avoid bacon, avocado, nuts, and full-fat cheeses. Replace soured cream or mayonnaise with low-fat yogurt.

PEPPERS ▷
Peppers contain no cholesterol or fat, and are low in sodium.

Peppers contain few carbohydrates

2 SEASONAL SALADS

When choosing a salad, take advantage of the seasons and serve ingredients that are at their peak of freshness and flavour. Tender young spinach and asparagus herald the spring, appearing in salads with hot bacon dressing or vinaigrette. In the summer months, choose salads that feature vine-ripened tomatoes or melons. Wonderful autumn salads can be made with fennel or pears, while in cold weather, a warming salad based on lentils is very welcome.

MELON ▷
Melons make a cool salad base for hot summer months, especially if mixed with cherry tomatoes.

SPINACH △
Make a spring salad from fresh young spinach, bacon, and a red wine vinegar dressing.

◁ FENNEL
Serve with sliced ripe pears, Gorgonzola dressing, and crunchy walnuts for an autumnal meal.

◁ RED CABBAGE
Combine red and white cabbage in a creamy coleslaw to serve with cold roast meats in the winter.

Seasonal ingredients

Spring	Summer	Autumn	Winter
Young spinach	Tomato	Fennel	Lentils
Lettuce	Melon	Pear	Chinese leaves
Asparagus	Avocado	Celeriac	White cabbage
New potato	Mango	Beetroot	Red cabbage
Spring onion	Cucumber	Lamb's lettuce	Chicory
Watercress	Peppers	Grapefruit	Celery

3 FIRST COURSE SALADS

There are no hard and fast rules as to when to serve a salad as a starter, and when as a main course. In general, simple salads make the best starters. Garden or Greek salad, autumn vegetable, leek or asparagus vinaigrette, mozzarella and tomato, Mediterranean, prawn and courgette, and coleslaw are all ideal salads to start a meal with.

AUTUMN VEGETABLE SALAD

MEDITERRANEAN SALAD

4 MAIN COURSE SALADS

Main course salads often contain meat or fish, and are more substantial in volume. Salad Niçoise, fresh tuna Niçoise, Waldorf chicken, pasta and mussel or scallop, tropical and teriyaki chicken, and wild rice and turkey all make excellent main courses. Serve them unaccompanied or with a simple side salad of lettuce and other greens tossed in a basic vinaigrette dressing.

SALAD NIÇOISE

SALAD INGREDIENTS

5 BASIC INGREDIENTS

Most of the recipes in this book feature the traditional round or cos lettuces, as well as green vegetables such as spinach or cabbage, but the range of ingredients that can be included is vast. Heighten the flavour of salads with fresh herbs. Include them in the dressing or mix in with the salad.

SALAD
ADDITIONS
Herbs, mushrooms, olives, fennel, and raisins can be added to a green salad.

6 BASIC EQUIPMENT

Salads need very little equipment to prepare, but a few basic items are vital. Use a sharp chef's knife for chopping, a thin-bladed knife for slicing fish and cucumber, and a small knife for cutting vegetables. Use a colander for draining vegetables, and a whisk to make dressings.

CHEF'S
KNIFE

THIN-
BLADED
KNIFE

SMALL
KNIFE

11

7 ESSENTIAL GREENS

The extensive range of salad greens available throughout the year means that you need never be short of exciting ingredients when making a leafy salad. Each combination produces its own taste, so always balance your ingredients for the best mixture of colour, taste, and texture to ensure a successful salad.

Cos ▷
The crisp texture and mild taste of cos mix well with strong flavours.

CHICORY △
(ENDIVE)
Crisp when raw, chicory combines well with avocado.

△ ICEBERG
Crunchy iceberg leaves are suitable for most salads.

◁ ESCAROLE
Also known as broad chicory or Batavian endive, escarole has a strong bite to it.

△ CURLY ENDIVE (CHICOREE FRISEE)
Curly endive has a peppery taste that spices up any salad.

RADICCHIO △
Radicchio keeps its sharp taste against the strongest of flavours.

△ **RED OAK LEAF**
The russet-coloured leaves of this lettuce add colour to any salad.

△ **FRISEE DE RUFFEE**
Like curly endive, frisée de ruffée has a slight peppery taste that contrasts well with other flavours.

△ **LAMB'S LETTUCE**
Delicately textured lamb's lettuce is the perfect complement to stronger greens.

ROCKET △
Pungent-tasting rocket is best served with strong-flavoured meat.

△ **WATERCRESS**
The strong mustard taste of watercress means that it should be used sparingly.

◁ **LOLLO ROSSO**
The distinctive taste of lollo rosso stands out against other flavours.

8 HOW TO WASH & DRY SALAD GREENS

Salad greens must be washed thoroughly to remove any grit or soil and to help make them crisp. Immerse the leaves in a bowl full of cold water and leave them for a few minutes. You can prepare salad greens in advance by wrapping them loosely in paper towels or a tea towel after washing and drying. Store in the refrigerator, 1–2 hours.

1 △ Agitate leaves to loosen any grit. Lift them out of the water and rinse under cold, running water.

2 ▷ Tear large leaves with your hands into two or three pieces. Dry leaves with a salad spinner or by patting them dry with a tea towel or a paper towel.

SALAD SPINNER

9 USING A SALAD SPINNER

Wet leaves dilute dressings and reduce the crispness of the finished salad, so make sure all leaves are completely dry after you have washed them. The best way to do this is in a basic salad spinner, which will dry them simply and effectively.

10 HOW TO CUT FRISEE LETTUCE

Cut deep into root end

Frisée, and lettuces such as cos, oak leaf, and curly endive, all have solid root ends that must be cut away from the leaves. Cut into the root end with a sharp knife and remove it completely. Discard both the root and the tough outer leaves. Then pull apart the inner leaves and wash them well, as they will have soil and dirt in between them. Dry the leaves thoroughly before serving.

11 HOW TO CORE A CHICORY

The chicory core can be bitter and should be discarded before the leaves are used in a salad. With a small, sharp knife, cut it out with a circular movement. Be careful not to damage the inner leaves.

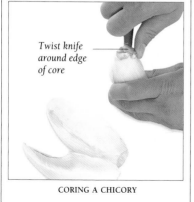

Twist knife around edge of core

CORING A CHICORY

12 HOW TO PREPARE GARLIC

To separate garlic cloves, crush the bulb with the heel of your hand. Then lightly crush each clove with the flat side of a chef's knife to loosen the skin. Peel off the skin with your fingers. Finely chop the garlic with a chef's knife by moving the blade back and forth.

CRUSHING GARLIC

13 ESSENTIAL HERBS

Fresh herbs will improve any salad, and can be added to complement or enhance the taste of the ingredients or as a garnish on the finished dish. All herbs are best picked fresh during the summer.

MINT ▷
Mint has a strong taste and can be used in sauces or as a garnish.

CHIVES ▷
A mild form of onion, chives should be added sparingly.

BASIL △
Rich and peppery, basil goes well with tomato dishes.

CORIANDER △
The leaves have a bitter and musky flavour.

PARSLEY ▷
Rich in vitamins and minerals, parsley is often used as a garnish.

TARRAGON ▷
Sweet and spicy, tarragon is ideal with chicken.

14 HOW TO CHOP HERBS

Most herbs are coarsely or finely chopped before they are added to other ingredients. Delicate herbs, such as tarragon, bruise easily, so do not chop them too much. Strip the leaves from the stalks and pile on a chopping board. Using both hands, pivot the knife blade back and forth until they are cut to the desired texture.

Use sharp knife to avoid bruising leaves

15 PEPPERS

All unripe peppers are green but ripen into many shades: the riper and more colourful the pepper, the sweeter and less assertive its taste. Peppers are enjoyed for their texture.

◁ **WHITE PEPPER**
Mild in taste, white pepper is an unusual addition to any salad.

PURPLE PEPPER ▷
Not widely available, purple peppers add colour to a salad.

△ **RED PEPPER**
Ripe red peppers are sweet and succulent.

△ **YELLOW PEPPER**
Yellow peppers are sweet in taste.

◁ **GREEN PEPPER**
Ripe green peppers have a sharp, grassy flavour.

16 HOW TO PREPARE A PEPPER

The only part of the pepper which cannot be eaten is the core. To remove the core, cut round the stalk and the core with a sharp knife. Grip the stalk firmly and twist it as you pull it away from the flesh. Slice the pepper into rings, or cut it in half, then slice into strips, or chop into dice.

1 ◁ To dice a pepper, cut it in half and scrape out the seeds. Then slice away any protruding white ribs.

2 △ Set each half pepper cut-side down and flatten it with the heel of your hand. Slice halves lengthwise into thin strips, and then cut strips into whatever size dice you require. Use a sharp chef's knife for quick and efficient work.

17 CHILLIES

Chilli peppers vary in flavour, and range in strength from mild to hot. As a general rule, the smaller the chilli, the hotter the flavour. Chillies are an acquired taste, and should be used sparingly, as their flavour will permeate all other ingredients.

△ **JALAPENO CHILLIES**
The rounded green jalapeño is one of the hottest chillies available.

SERRANO CHILLIES ▷
Like all small chillies, the red serrano is hot and will overwhelm every other flavour.

△ **HOT GREEN CHILLIES**
Remove the seeds and ribs from this chilli to cool its hot taste.

18 HOW TO PREPARE A CHILLI

Add chillies to vinaigrette dressings to spice up bean and other salads. If the chilli is hot, remove the seeds and ribs, which are the hottest parts. As a safety precaution, always wear rubber gloves when handling fresh or dried chillies, as they contain volatile oils which can irritate or burn your skin and eyes.

1 Cut the chilli in half lengthwise. Scoop out the seeds and white ribs.

2 Cut the halves into thin strips with a small, sharp knife.

3 Gather the strips together and cut across into very fine dice.

19 TOMATOES

Along with the salad greens, tomatoes form the mainstay of many salads, adding taste and colour to the meal, as well as a decorative garnish to the finished dish.

△ **COMMON TOMATO**
Cut tomatoes into segments before serving.

△ **PLUM TOMATO**
Plum tomatoes have meaty flesh and a sweet taste.

△ **CHERRY TOMATOES**
Serve small, sweet cherry tomatoes whole or in halves.

◁ **BEEFSTEAK TOMATO**
The suitably named beefsteak tomato is best served in slices.

20 HOW TO PEEL A TOMATO

The only way to peel the skin off a tomato without bruising its flesh is to immerse it first in boiling water. Leave the tomato in the water for up to 15 seconds depending on its ripeness. As soon as the skin curls away from the flesh, remove it and, when cooled, peel away the rest of the skin with your fingers or a small knife.

1 With a paring knife, carefully cut out the core of the tomato.

2 Score bottom of tomato and immerse in boiling water.

3 Remove after 8–15 seconds, leave to cool, and peel away skin.

21 ESSENTIAL VEGETABLES

Vegetables feature in a number of salad recipes. Root vegetables, such as potatoes, should be boiled before a dressing is added, but carrots and mushrooms may appear either raw or cooked. Cucumber, celery, and spring onions are all eaten raw.

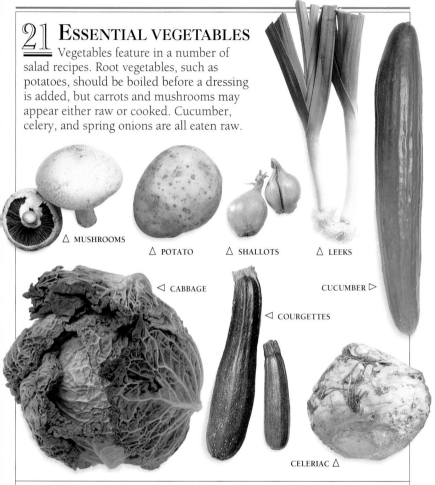

△ MUSHROOMS

△ POTATO

△ SHALLOTS

△ LEEKS

◁ CABBAGE

CUCUMBER ▷

◁ COURGETTES

CELERIAC △

22 HOW TO PREPARE BEETROOT

Beetroot is usually cooked before eating. Bring a saucepan of cold water to the boil. Wash the beetroot, and cook until tender when tested with the tip of a knife (about 1–1½ hours, depending on size). Drain the beetroot and let it cool. When it is cool, peel away the skin with your fingers, and trim the roots and tops.

23 HOW TO CHOP A SHALLOT

Separate the shallot into sections. For standard slices, cut into pieces that are about 3 mm (⅛ in) thick. For a fine chop, make the slices of shallot as thin as possible.

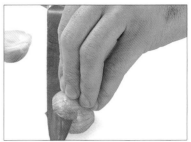

1 △ Peel the outer, papery skin from the shallot. Set it on a chopping board, hold it steady with your fingers, and slice horizontally towards the root.

2 ◁ Slice vertically through the shallot, leaving the root end uncut. Then cut across the shallot to make as fine dice as you require.

24 HOW TO PREPARE CARROTS

Raw carrots are an important part of many salads, either mixed with other ingredients or used as a garnish. You can refrigerate peeled carrots to keep them fresh.

GRATED CARROTS
Trim and peel each carrot before grating along the coarse side of the grater.

CARROT CURLS
Peel curls from the sides of the carrot with a vegetable curler.

25 MEAT IN SALADS

Add meat to a salad to make it more filling. Slivers of poached chicken, smoked turkey or marinated chicken breast, slices of hot sausage, thin strips of marinated rump steak, slices of Parma or smoked Westphalian ham, and chopped bacon rashers can all be used to good effect with salad vegetables to create a satisfying meal.

TERIYAKI CHICKEN

26 FISH IN SALADS

Like meat, use fish in a salad to add substance as well as flavour. Salmon, trout, monkfish, and tuna can be poached, fried, or grilled, while shellfish, such as scallops, prawns, and mussels should be boiled or sautéed. Marinades can be used to heighten the taste. Fish, such as anchovy, has a strong taste, so always add it sparingly so that it does not overwhelm the other ingredients.

FRESH TUNA SALAD NIÇOISE

27 NUTS IN SALADS

Add nuts to salads to give a distinctive crunchy texture. Toasted walnuts, hazelnuts, almonds, and pecans, and shelled, roasted, unsalted peanuts are just some of the different varieties that can be included. Most nuts can be eaten raw, or you can toast or roast them to bring out their full, woody flavour.

FESTIVE WILD RICE SALAD

28 CHEESE IN SALADS

Cheeses such as Parmesan, feta, and mozzarella, and blue varieties, including Gorgonzola, Stilton, and Danish blue, give a salty bite to any salad. Add cheese sparingly, otherwise its dominant taste will overwhelm the flavours of the other ingredients.

△ MOZZARELLA
Sliced, soft mozzarella is the ideal accompaniment to slices of plum tomato.

△ RICOTTA
A fresh cheese like ricotta can be mixed with herbs or nuts and served with lettuce.

△ PARMESAN
Grate hard cheeses such as Parmesan and sprinkle them on top of a salad.

29 HOW TO SHELL AN EGG

Chopped, sliced, or sieved hard-boiled eggs make an attractive addition to any salad, either as a main ingredient or as a garnish. To hard-boil an egg, place it in a saucepan with enough cold water to cover it. Bring the water to the boil and simmer for 10 minutes.

1 Once cooked, submerge the egg in cold water. Then roll or tap it on a flat surface to crack the shell all over.

2 Remove the shell carefully without damaging the white. Rinse with cold water and dry with a paper towel.

30 PASTA IN SALADS

The soft, doughy texture of pasta adds bulk and complements stronger tasting ingredients such as fish or meat that are mixed with it. Serve with a well-flavoured herb vinaigrette dressing to sharpen the overall taste, and as a final touch sprinkle with Parmesan cheese.

△ CONCHIGLIE

FUSILLI ▷

△ PENNE

FARFALLE ▷

31 FRUIT IN SALADS

Citrus fruits, particularly lemons, provide a delicious acidity to a salad, but almost any fruit makes a refreshing addition. Try fresh figs, apples, raspberries, mangoes, and melons (*see p.47 on how to preserve fresh fruit*).

◁ GRAPEFRUIT
The sharp taste of grapefruit combines well with the mild flesh of avocado.

FIGS ▽
The sweetness of fresh figs marries perfectly with savoury flavours, such as cheese.

△ APPLE
Slices of crunchy apple complement crisp lettuce leaves and cucumber slices.

△ MANGO
Add cubes of mango to chicken dishes.

32 HOW TO CUT AN AVOCADO

Before you start to slice an avocado, you must first remove both the stone and the skin. Begin by cutting lengthwise around the avocado through to the stone. Then remove the stone with a sharp chef's knife (*see below*) or a spoon. Strip away the skin with a knife.

1 Twist the avocado with both hands to loosen the halves and pull them apart gently.

2 With a sharp tap, embed the knife blade in the stone and twist it free of the flesh.

3 Cut the avocado into quarters and strip off the skin, using a small sharp knife.

33 HOW TO SEED GRAPES

Many varieties of seedless grapes are now available, but if you can only find the seeded kind, remove the seeds before serving in a salad.

SEEDING GRAPES
Halve each grape and flick out the seeds with the tip of a small knife.

34 HOW TO SEGMENT CITRUS FRUIT

To segment a grapefruit or orange, cut away both ends of the fruit. Set it upright and, working from top to bottom, cut away the zest, pith, and skin. Then slide a knife down each side of a segment and cut it away from the membrane.

PEELED & SEGMENTED FRUIT

HOW TO DRESS A SALAD

35 CHOOSING THE RIGHT DRESSING

Matching the dressing to the ingredients is the secret of a successful salad. As a basic rule, use a delicate vinaigrette dressing for subtle, mild flavours, and a much stronger, more spirited dressing for robust flavours.

36 WHICH VINEGAR?

Choose from red or white wine vinegar, sherry vinegar, cider vinegar, rice wine vinegar, or even Champagne vinegar when making up a vinaigrette. Balsamic vinegar gives dressing a robust, fruit flavour, or use a wine vinegar flavoured with herbs and spices.

BALSAMIC VINEGAR CHAMPAGNE VINEGAR WINE VINEGARS

37 HOW TO MAKE HERB VINEGAR

To make 750 ml (1¼ pints) vinegar

Ingredients
*1 bunch fresh tarragon or basil,
or 5–7 sprigs of fresh rosemary or thyme,
or any combination of herbs
750 ml (1¼ pints) white wine vinegar*

1 Lay herbs on chopping board and bruise them by pounding 5–6 times with rolling pin to draw out flavour. Put herbs in sterilized jar.
2 Bring vinegar just to the boil and pour over herbs. Let cool, seal jar, and leave in cool place for at least 2 weeks.
3 Strain vinegar through muslin or paper coffee filters into new jar.

38 WHICH OIL?

Each oil has its own distinctive flavour. Match the type of oil to your salad ingredients. Groundnut oil is light, olive oil has a rich flavour, hazelnut and walnut are nutty, and safflower and sunflower are almost flavourless. Combine oils such as safflower and hazelnut for a milder taste.

△ EXTRA-VIRGIN OLIVE OILS
Olive oil is graded according to its level of acidity. Extra-virgin has the lowest level, virgin oil the highest.

◁ INFUSED OLIVE OILS
Some Italian extra-virgin oils are infused with truffles or lemon. French oils are often mixed with herbs.

39 HOW TO MAKE HERB OIL

To make 750 ml (1¼ pints) oil

Ingredients
1 bunch fresh tarragon or basil, or 5-7 sprigs of fresh rosemary or thyme
750 ml (1¼ pints) extra-virgin olive oil

1 Lay herbs on chopping board and bruise them by pounding 5–6 times with rolling pin to draw out their full flavour. Put herbs in clean glass bottle or sealable jar.
2 Pour oil into jar, seal, and leave to infuse in a cool place before serving, 1–2 weeks.

40 HOW TO MAKE VINAIGRETTE

The standard recipe for vinaigrette dressing follows the principle of one part vinegar to three parts oil, but these quantities can vary according to taste and the other ingredients that are used. Add fresh herbs, such as rosemary or thyme, to this simple base.

1 In a small bowl, whisk together 60 ml (4 tbsp) vinegar with salt and pepper. If you want to add extra bite to the dressing, mix in 10 ml (2 tsp) Dijon or other kind of mustard.

2 Gradually whisk in 180 ml (12 tbsp) oil in a steady stream so that the vinaigrette dressing emulsifies and begins to thicken slightly. Season the finished dressing according to taste.

41 STORING VINAIGRETTE

A basic vinaigrette of oil, vinegar, mustard, and seasoning will stay fresh for up to one week in a sealed container at room temperature. When you are ready to use it, decant the dressing into another container, add flavourings as required.

42 WHAT TO ADD TO A VINAIGRETTE

EXTRA-VIRGIN OLIVE OIL

Apart from herbs, such as rosemary, thyme, mint, oregano, chives, parsley, or tarragon, there are many other ingredients that can be added to flavour a basic vinaigrette dressing. Garlic, shallots, chillies, horseradish, nuts, honey, seeds, and berry purée can all be employed to good effect.

43 CHILLI DRESSING

To make 250 ml (9 fl oz) dressing

Ingredients
125 ml (4 fl oz)
cider vinegar
2.5 ml (½ tsp) ground cumin
3 fresh green chillies
1 bunch fresh coriander
125 ml (4 fl oz) safflower oil

1 Whisk together vinegar, cumin, salt, and pepper.
2 Prepare chillies (see p.18); add to other ingredients. Chop coriander.
3 Gradually whisk in safflower oil so that vinaigrette emulsifies.
4 Add coriander to dressing.

44 SPICY SOY DRESSING

To make 275 ml (½ pint) dressing

Ingredients
2 cm (¾ in) root ginger
2 chillies; 2 garlic cloves
10 ml (2 tsp) sugar
60 ml (4 tbsp) rice
wine vinegar
125 ml (4 fl oz) soy sauce
60 ml (4 tbsp) groundnut oil
30 ml (2 tbsp) sesame oil

1 ◁ Peel skin from fresh ginger; slice, crush, and chop into fine dice. Prepare chillies (see p.18) and garlic (p.15). Add to sugar, vinegar, and pepper in bowl. Pour in soy sauce.

2 ▽ Gradually whisk in groundnut and sesame oils so that dressing emulsifies and thickens. Season to taste.

Whisk as you pour in groundnut oil

Sesame oil adds nutty flavour to dressing

45 POPPY SEED DRESSING
To make 200 ml (7 fl oz)

Ingredients
½ small onion
45 ml (3 tbsp) vinegar
15 ml (1 tbsp) honey
Mustard & ginger
150 ml (5 fl oz) oil
15 ml (1 tbsp) poppy seeds

1 ▷ Grate onion into bowl. Add vinegar, honey, 2.5 ml (½ tsp) mustard powder, 1.25 ml (¼ tsp) ground ginger. Whisk together vigorously. Season.

2 ◁ Gradually whisk in vegetable oil so the vinaigrette emulsifies and thickens. Add poppy seeds to the bowl and whisk together. Taste for seasoning.

46 MAYONNAISE
To make 375ml (12 fl oz)

Ingredients
2 egg yolks
30 ml (2 tbsp) white
wine vinegar, or
15 ml (1 tbsp) lemon juice
5 ml (1 tsp) Dijon mustard
300 ml (½ pint) peanut or
olive oil

1 In a small bowl, whisk egg yolks until thick with half the vinegar or lemon juice, and mustard if using. Season to taste.

2 Add oil drop by drop, whisking constantly. After 30 ml (2 tbsp), slowly pour in rest of oil and vinegar. Season.

47 WHAT TO ADD TO MAYONNAISE

Mayonnaise is the basic ingredient of a range of dressings. Add ketchup, chilli sauce, green pepper, pimento, and chives to create thousand island dressing, and chopped gherkins, shallots, capers, parsley, and tarragon to make tartare sauce. Garlic, double cream, or finely chopped spinach, watercress, or parsley leaves, all add flavour to a simple mayonnaise.

BLUE CHEESE
Add crumbled blue cheese to mayonnaise.

48 RASPBERRY DRESSING

To make 200 ml (7 fl oz)

Ingredients
75 g (2½ oz) fresh raspberries
75 ml (5 tbsp) raspberry vinegar
75 ml (5 tbsp) mayonnaise
30 ml (2 tbsp) double cream
15 ml (1 tbsp) hazelnut oil

MAKING PUREE
Do not waste any raspberry purée clinging to the bottom of the sieve.

1 Wash raspberries if dirty. Work the raspberries through sieve over a bowl, pressing with back of spoon to make a purée. Scrape pulp clinging to sieve into bowl.
2 Add vinegar, mayonnaise, cream, and oil to purée. Whisk until combined; season to taste.

49 RUSSIAN DRESSING

Russian dressing used to include caviar, hence its name, and is served with salads, fish, and cold meat. To 375 ml (12 fl oz) mayonnaise, add 60 ml (4 tbsp) tomato ketchup, 1 chopped shallot, 60 ml (4 tbsp) chopped pickled gherkin, 5 ml (1 tsp) grated horseradish, and a few drops of Tabasco sauce. Season.

50 Salad Cream

From northern Europe and the United States come a group of salad dressings which, unlike mayonnaise or vinaigrette, are based on milk or cream rather than oil. The most common of these is the English salad cream. To make this, sieve 2 hard-boiled egg yolks into a bowl. Stir in 1 raw egg yolk and 5 ml (1 tsp) water. Add 125 ml (4 fl oz) double cream in a slow, steady stream, stirring constantly. Season to taste with salt and pepper. Flavour with 15 ml (1 tbsp) of lemon juice or a flavoured vinegar.

51 Soured Cream Dressing

To make 725 ml (1¼ pints)

Ingredients
30 ml (2 tbsp) sugar
250 ml (8 fl oz) soured cream
175 ml (6 fl oz) vinegar
10 ml (2 tsp) mustard
10 ml (2 tsp) caraway seeds
250 ml (8 fl oz) mayonnaise

1 ◁ Put sugar, soured cream, and vinegar in a bowl. Add mustard and caraway seeds. Season to taste. The soured cream will thicken the dressing.

Mustard powder spices up the dressing

Caraway seeds add texture

2 ◁ Whisk the ingredients together until combined thoroughly. Add the mayonnaise to the soured cream dressing and whisk well again. Season according to taste.

52 CACIK

To make 725 ml (1¼ pints)

Ingredients

2 small cucumbers, about 500 g (1 lb)
3 garlic cloves
1 bunch fresh mint
2.5 ml (½ tsp) ground coriander
1.25 ml (¼ tsp) ground cumin
500 ml (16 fl oz) plain yogurt

TZATZIKI
The Greek version of cacik is called tzatziki. To make tzatziki, prepare the ingredients as for cacik, using 1 small cucumber and, in place of chopped mint, use 1 small bunch of fresh, finely chopped dill.

MINT

1 ▷ Peel and trim cucumbers; cut lengthwise in half. Scoop out seeds, and cut into fine dice. Transfer cucumbers to colander, sprinkle with salt, and stir to mix. Leave 15–20 minutes. Finely chop garlic; coarsely chop mint leaves.

2 △ Put cucumbers in bowl. Add garlic, mint, coriander, cumin, yogurt. Stir well. Season to taste. Chill in refrigerator for 2 hours.

53 BOILED DRESSING

To make American boiled dressing, mix 20 g (¾ oz) flour, 5 ml (1 tsp) mustard powder, 15 ml (½ oz) sugar, a pinch of cayenne, and 2 egg yolks in a heavy pan. Stir in 20 g (¾ oz) melted butter, 175 ml (6 fl oz) milk, and 60 ml (4 tbsp) wine vinegar. Heat until thickened over low heat, whisking constantly.

CLASSIC SALADS

54 COLOURFUL GARDEN SALAD
Serves 8

Ingredients
1 head radicchio,
about 150 g (5 oz)
2 heads chicory, about 150 g (5 oz)
1 small head frisée,
about 300 g (10 oz)
125 g (4 oz) lamb's lettuce
125 g (4 oz) rocket
5–7 sprigs fresh parsley
5–7 sprigs fresh basil
5–7 sprigs fresh tarragon
1 small bunch fresh chives
Vinaigrette dressing
Edible flowers (optional)

1 Discard any withered outer leaves
from radicchio. Cut away root end.
Separate, wash, and dry leaves. Cut out
and discard core from each chicory and
slice leaves diagonally. Cut off frisée
root, discard outer leaves and pull apart.

2 With your fingers, pinch away any
root ends from lamb's lettuce,
keeping small bunches of leaves intact.
Wash and dry all the salad leaves. Nip
parsley, basil, and tarragon tips from
stalks. Strip leaves from stalks.

3 Remove flowers from chives and
cut in 2.5 cm (1 in) lengths. Place
salad leaves in a large bowl and mix
together. Add herbs to salad. Prepare
vinaigrette dressing (see p.28), whisk
well, and pour over salad.

4 Toss salad thoroughly: lift a portion of greens and let them fall; turn bowl slightly and repeat until greens are evenly coated. Taste salad to ensure seasoning is well balanced.

55 EDIBLE FLOWERS

Some flowers are toxic, so eat only store-bought specimens or, if picking your own, select known edible flowers, such as honeysuckle or marigold, grown without the use of pesticides or other sprays.

PANSY

NASTURTIUM

BORAGE

TO SERVE
Add any edible flowers and serve the salad at once, while the leaves are fresh.

35

56 HOW TO CHOP TOMATOES

Always choose the ripest tomatoes available to achieve the best flavour. Wash the tomatoes carefully. With the tip of a small knife, core each one. Cut it into eight wedges, then cut each wedge in half. These tomato wedges are bite-sized and will combine colourfully with other ingredients, especially in a Greek salad.

57 GREEK SALAD

Serves 6–8

Ingredients

2 small cucumbers
2 green peppers
1 medium red onion
175 g (6 oz) feta cheese
1 kg (2 lb) tomatoes
Herb vinaigrette dressing
125 g (4 oz) olives

1 Peel cucumbers. Trim and cut each cucumber lengthwise in half. Scoop out seeds with spoon. Cut halves into 1.25 cm (½ in) pieces.

2 Cut, pull out, and discard each pepper core. Halve peppers, scrape out seeds, and cut away white ribs. Cut into small pieces.

3 Peel and trim red onion. Cut thin slice from one side so it sits firmly on chopping board. Cut onion crosswise into thin rings.

4 Cut feta cheese and tomatoes into chunks.

5 Put tomatoes, cucumbers, peppers, and onion rings in a bowl. Prepare herb dressing (*see p.28*) with oil, parsley, mint, oregano, and red wine vinegar; pour over salad.

6 With a large spoon, toss vegetables in dressing. Add olives and feta cheese and gently toss again.

TO SERVE
Allow the flavours to mellow for about 30 minutes before serving.

58 ADDING OLIVES TO A SALAD

Olives are an essential element of Greek and other salads, adding essential bite and substance to the accompanying ingredients. In Greece, olives are left whole in salads, but you may prefer to stone them, using an olive stoner.

GREEN OLIVES ▷
Green olives are picked unripe and soaked before they are brined (salted).

◁ **BLACK OLIVES**
Black olives are fully ripened fruit that are brined straight away.

59 MOZZARELLA & PLUM TOMATO
Serves 4–6

Ingredients
500 g (1 lb) mozzarella cheese
6 plum tomatoes
1 small cucumber
Herb vinaigrette dressing

1 Cut mozzarella cheese into thin slices.
2 Core tomatoes and cut each one crosswise into six plump slices.
3 Peel cucumber and cut into small dice.
4 Make herb vinaigrette dressing with basil, garlic, olive oil, and red wine vinegar (*see p.28*).
5 Arrange alternating slices of mozzarella and tomato on individual plates. Set cucumber dice in a small cluster in centre of each serving. Whisk dressing and spoon over salad.
6 Leave for 20 minutes before serving.

TO SERVE
Add fresh basil leaves to complement the textures of cheese and tomato.

37

60 COLESLAW
Serves 8–10

Ingredients
500 g (1 lb) medium
carrots
1 white cabbage, about
1.4 kg (3 lb)
1 medium onion
Soured cream
dressing

TO SERVE
Divide the salad among
individual bowls, and
garnish each serving with
carrot curls for added
colour and contrast.

1 Trim and peel carrots. Using coarse side of grater, grate all but one carrot. Use vegetable peeler to peel curls from length of remaining carrot. Trim cabbage and discard any wilted leaves. Cut into quarters, remove core, and shred into thin slices. Mix grated carrot and shredded cabbage in a bowl.

2 Peel, slice, and cut onion into fine dice. Add onion to carrot and cabbage and mix well. Prepare soured cream dressing (*see p.32*) and pour over salad. Stir until thoroughly coated. Cover, and chill in refrigerator for at least 4 hours so that the flavours mellow. Taste salad for seasoning.

61 APPLE & PINEAPPLE COLESLAW
Serves 8–10

Ingredients
4 tart dessert apples
625 g (1¼ lb) can crushed pineapple
1 white cabbage, about 1.4 kg (3 lb)
Buttermilk dressing

1 Grate four unpeeled apples. Drain pineapple. Mix together in a large bowl.
2 Shred cabbage and add to bowl.
3 Make a buttermilk dressing with 150 ml (5 fl oz) cider vinegar, 10 ml (2 tsp) mustard powder, 250 ml (8 fl oz) buttermilk, 250 ml (8 fl oz) bottled mayonnaise. Season.
4 Pour dressing on salad. Stir. Chill for 4 hours.

62 RED & WHITE CABBAGE COLESLAW
Serves 8–10

Ingredients
1.4 kg (3 lb) white cabbage
1 medium onion
750 g (1½ lb) red cabbage
Buttermilk dressing

1 Shred white cabbage into thin slices. Cut onion into fine dice.
2 Shred red cabbage. Heat large saucepan of salted water to boiling. Add red cabbage, bring back to boil and simmer for 1 minute.
3 Drain red cabbage. While still hot, sprinkle with 60 ml (4 tbsp) red wine vinegar.
4 Make buttermilk dressing as above, with juice of three lemons in place of vinegar.
5 Combine red and white cabbage in a bowl. Pour dressing over salad. Stir well, and season to taste.
6 Chill 4 hours.

TO SERVE
Serve on a large platter with cold turkey or beef.

63 AUTUMN VEGETABLE
Serves 6

Ingredients
500 g (1 lb) carrots
45 ml (3 tbsp) cider vinegar
5 ml (1 tsp) sugar
75 ml (5 tbsp) vegetable oil
90 g (3 oz) raisins
750 g (1½ lb) celeriac
175 ml (6 fl oz) bottled mayonnaise
30 ml (2 tbsp) Dijon mustard, more if needed

1 Peel and trim carrots. Grate coarsely.
2 Make dressing by whisking vinegar and sugar in a bowl. Slowly whisk in oil. Season to taste.
3 Add carrots and raisins to dressing. Toss together, and chill in refrigerator for 1 hour.
4 Peel celeriac and cut into thin strips; place in saucepan of cold, salted water and bring to boil. Simmer 1–2 minutes, then drain well.
5 In a large bowl, combine mayonnaise and mustard. Season to taste.
6 Add celeriac to mustard dressing. Chill 1 hour.

TO SERVE
Place celeriac and carrot and raisin side by side.

64 BEETROOT & CELERIAC

Serves 6

Ingredients

500 g (1 lb) fresh beetroot
45 ml (3 tbsp) cider vinegar
5 ml (1 tsp) sugar
75 ml (5 tbsp) vegetable oil
10 ml (2 tsp) caraway seeds
750 g (1½ lb) celeriac
175 ml (6 fl oz) bottled mayonnaise
30 ml (2 tbsp) fresh or bottled horseradish

1 △ Wash beetroot; do not peel. Bring saucepan of cold water to boil, add beetroot, and cook until tender, 40–50 minutes. Drain, and when cool, peel off skin. Mix vinegar, sugar, oil, and seeds to make dressing. Season.

2 ◁ Coarsely grate beetroot. Add dressing; toss gently. Cut celeriac into thin strips; place in saucepan of cold, salted water. Bring to boil; simmer 1–2 minutes. Drain well, and mix with mayonnaise and horseradish. Season.

TO SERVE
Arrange beetroot and celeriac in alternating curves on a large serving plate.

41

65 LEEKS VINAIGRETTE
Serves 4–6

Ingredients
6 medium leeks, about 1 kg (2 lb)
45 ml (3 tbsp) white wine vinegar
5 ml (1 tsp) Dijon mustard
175 ml (6 fl oz) safflower oil
2 shallots
1 egg for garnish
5–7 sprigs parsley for garnish

TO SERVE
Serve with a garnish of parsley, egg white, and sieved egg yolk, known as mimosa because of its resemblance to the blossom.

1 △ Trim leeks, discarding roots and tops. Halve each leek lengthwise, leaving them attached at root end. Wash thoroughly. Divide into two bundles; tie together at each end. Add to boiling water; simmer for 15–25 minutes.

2 △ When leeks are tender, drain, rinse in cold water, and dry. Cut leeks into 7.5 cm (3 in) lengths. Remove string. Prepare dressing by mixing vinegar and mustard in a bowl. Add oil. Dice shallots and add. Season.

3 △ Lay leeks in a shallow dish. Briskly whisk dressing and pour over leeks. Cover; leave to marinate in refrigerator for 1 hour. Hard-boil and shell egg. Cut in half and separate white from yolk. Coarsely chop the white. Work yolk through a sieve into a bowl.

4 △ Arrange leeks on plates. Finely chop parsley and spread on sheet of greaseproof paper. Scoop parsley onto edge of chef's knife blade; holding blade diagonally, tap it so that parsley drops in neat line. Repeat with yolk and white.

66 PREPARING ASPARAGUS

If the asparagus is young and the stalks slender, the stalks will not need peeling before cooking. If the stalks are tough, strip away the rough outer skin and trim off the woody ends.

ASPARAGUS

67 ASPARAGUS VINAIGRETTE

Trim 1 kg (2 lb) asparagus spears. Tie into 4–6 bundles and add to boiling water. Simmer for 5–7 minutes until tender. Prepare dressing as for leeks vinaigrette (see p.42), using sherry vinegar in place of white wine vinegar. Garnish with egg yolk and white.

ASPARAGUS VINAIGRETTE

68 AVOCADO & PARMA HAM
Serves 4

Ingredients
4 grapefruit
125 g (4 oz) thinly sliced
Parma ham
175 g (6 oz) rocket
2 avocados
Poppy seed dressing

TO SERVE
*Sprinkle thin grapefruit strips
and dressing on each serving.*

1 △ With vegetable peeler, pare half of
the peel from one grapefruit. Cut into
thin strips; simmer in hot water for 2
minutes. Cut away skin from other fruit.

2 △ Holding each peeled grapefruit
over a bowl, slide a knife down
each segment to cut it free from the
membranes. Release segments into a
bowl. Discard seeds as you go. Cut
ham slices into 2.5 cm (1 in) strips.

3 △ Separate rocket leaves; rinse, drain, and dry well. Prepare avocados (*see p.25*) and cut lengthwise into thin slices. Brush slices with acidic grapefruit juice to prevent them discolouring (*see p.47*). Set aside.

4 △ Prepare dressing (*see p.30*). Toss rocket leaves with one-third dressing; arrange on plate with slices of avocado and grapefruit segments. Curl ham into cones, arrange in centre. Spoon over rest of dressing.

69 AVOCADO & SMOKED SALMON
Serves 4

Ingredients
*Poppy seed dressing; 5 sprigs fresh dill
4 grapefruit; 2 avocados
175 g (6 oz) sliced smoked salmon
1 small head radicchio, about 90 g (3 oz)
90 g (3 oz) rocket*

TO SERVE
*Garnish with sprigs of fresh dill.
Add extra dressing to taste.*

1 Prepare dressing (*see p.30*) and whisk in finely chopped dill leaves.
2 Segment grapefruit; slice avocados.
3 Cut salmon into 5 cm (2 in) strips.
4 Cut root end from radicchio and discard withered leaves. Separate leaves, wash, and dry well.
5 Separate, wash, and dry rocket leaves. Toss rocket and radicchio in dressing and alternate on plate.
6 Arrange grapefruit and avocado on top. Curl salmon into rose in centre.

45

70 PEAR, FENNEL, & WALNUT

Serves 6

Ingredients

60 g (2 oz) walnut pieces

125 g (4 oz) Gorgonzola cheese

60 ml (4 tbsp) red wine vinegar

75 ml (5 tbsp) olive oil

1 large fennel bulb, about 375 g (12 oz)

3 ripe pears, about 625 g (1¼ lb)

1 lemon

1 Toast walnuts on baking sheet in oven at 180° C/350° F/gas 4 for 5–8 minutes until crisp.

2 Cut rind from Gorgonzola and crumble cheese with fingers. Put two-thirds of cheese in a bowl with red wine vinegar. Slowly whisk in oil so that dressing emulsifies and thickens slightly. Add rest of cheese. Season to taste.

3 Trim stalks and tough outer pieces from fennel and cut into thin lengthwise slices.

4 Peel pears, cut in half, and scoop out core.

5 Cut pears into thin slices and squeeze lemon juice over each of the slices to prevent discolouration.

6 Alternate pear and fennel slices on plates. Spoon on walnuts and Gorgonzola dressing.

TO SERVE
Garnish with fennel fronds to add a touch of colour.

71 HOW TO KEEP FRUIT FRESH

Fruit such as pears, apples, and avocados quickly lose their colour when they are cut up for inclusion in a salad. Brush each slice of fruit with the acidic juice of a lemon, orange, or grapefruit to prevent discolouration and keep the fruit fresh and attractive. Make sure each slice is well coated on both sides with juice.

72 TANGY MELON
Serves 6

Ingredients
1 large orange or yellow melon, about 1.4 kg (3 lb)
2 small green melons, about 1.4 kg (3 lb)
½ red onion; 1 orange
250 ml (8 fl oz) plain yogurt
15 ml (1 tbsp) honey

1 Cut large melon lengthwise in half. Scoop out and discard seeds. Cut each half into three wedges. Cut the flesh from the shell, leaving wedges intact, and slice each wedge into 2.5 cm (1 in) chunks. Push each chunk slightly off-centre to create a decorative pattern on the shell.
2 Halve and seed green melons. Cut one half into a decorative container for dressing; scoop balls from rest. Chill in refrigerator.
3 Cut half the red onion into fine dice. Cut away skin and pith from orange following curve of fruit. Working over a bowl to catch juice, cut out orange segments by slicing down each side of segment to free it from membranes. Scoop out each segment.
4 Whisk yogurt with honey and orange juice to make dressing. Transfer to melon container. Garnish with parsley.

TO SERVE
Arrange ingredients on a serving platter around the container of dressing.

73 SPRINGTIME RICE
Serves 4–6

Ingredients
1 lemon
200 g (7 oz) long-grain rice
250 g (8 oz) young
asparagus
3 celery sticks

250 g (8 oz) sliced
smoked salmon
45 ml (3 tbsp)
tarragon vinegar
10 ml (2 tsp) Dijon mustard
175 ml (6 fl oz) safflower oil

1 ◁ Boil saucepan of salted water. Add juice from half a lemon; drop in lemon shell. Pour in rice; simmer for 18–20 minutes. Drain well. Strip outer skin from asparagus and trim off woody ends. Simmer until tender for 5–7 minutes. Trim tips; cut stalks into 1.25 cm (½ in) pieces.

2 △ Peel strings from celery sticks. Cut each stick lengthwise into 7.5 cm (3 in) long pieces, then cut each piece lengthwise into 2–3 strips. Stack strips and cut crosswise to make dice.

3 △ With a chef's knife, cut smoked salmon slices crosswise into 1.25 cm (½ in) strips. Prepare dressing by mixing vinegar and mustard; slowly whisk in oil. Season to taste.

4 ◁ Pour all but 30 ml (2 tbsp) of dressing over rice. Add chopped asparagus, celery, salmon, and juice from half a lemon. Toss ingredients together and season. Chill for 1 hour.

TO SERVE
Serve in bowls. Garnish with asparagus tips and brush with remaining dressing.

74 RICE VARIATIONS

Rice is an excellent base for many salads. If you can't obtain smoked salmon, try strips of smoked trout or another kind of fish. Peas or beans can be used instead of the asparagus, while cherry tomatoes add a splash of colour to any rice salad.

75 WILD RICE & TURKEY

Serves 8

Ingredients

375 g (12 oz) wild rice
175 g (6 oz) cranberries
60 ml (4 tbsp) sugar
60 g (2 oz) pecans
1 orange
2 shallots
60 ml (4 tbsp) cider vinegar
125 ml (4 fl oz)
safflower oil
375 g (12 oz) cooked turkey

1 Boil 1.5 litre (2¾ pints) salted water. Stir in wild rice, cover, and simmer until tender for about 1 hour. Drain well.

2 Spread cranberries in a baking dish, sprinkle with sugar, and bake in heated oven 190° C/ 375° F/gas 5 until they start to pop; 10–15 minutes for fresh fruit, less for defrosted fruit.

3 Bake pecans on baking sheet in heated oven 180° C/350° F/gas 4 until crisp, 5–8 minutes.

4 Pare zest from orange with vegetable peeler; cut into fine strips. Add to boiling water and simmer for 2 minutes. Drain and chop into fine grains. Squeeze juice from orange. Set aside.

5 Peel shallots; cut into fine dice. Mix vinegar, shallots, and orange juice. Whisk in oil so dressing emulsifies and thickens slightly. Season to taste. Transfer cranberries to dressing, leaving juice behind. Stir well.

6 Cut turkey into 1.25 cm (½ in) diagonal strips.

7 Add orange zest, two-thirds of cranberry dressing, and chopped pecans to rice. Toss well. Season to taste.

TO SERVE
Place rice on large plate with turkey in centre. Spoon over rest of dressing.

76 HOW TO PREPARE KIDNEY BEANS

Soak dried kidney beans in cold water overnight. Drain; rinse well. Put into large saucepan, cover well with cold water, and bring to boil, leaving pan uncovered. Boil for 10 minutes to get rid of toxins.

Drain, return to pan with peeled onion and a bouquet garni. Cover with cold water. Cover pan; simmer for up to 1½ hours until beans are tender. Add salt after cooking; if added before it will toughen beans.

77 TWO BEANS WITH GUACAMOLE
Serves 6–8

Ingredients
175 g (6 oz) red beans
175 g (6 oz) white beans
2 bouquet garnis
2 clove-studded onions
Chilli dressing
750 g (1½ lb) tomatoes
1 red & 1 green pepper
1 garlic clove
3 avocados
4–5 drops Tabasco sauce
1 lime

1 Soak dried red kidney beans and dried white kidney beans separately. Cook beans separately, each with a bouquet garni and clove-studded onion.
2 Prepare chilli dressing (*see p.29*).
3 Drain beans, rinse well in hot water, and while beans are still hot, combine with dressing in large bowl. Mix well. Leave to cool.
4 Peel and core tomatoes. Chop in small pieces.
5 Core and seed peppers. Dice. Add peppers and tomatoes to beans. Mix well.
6 Peel and chop garlic clove. Scrape avocado flesh from skin and combine with garlic by mashing avocado against side of bowl with fork. Add pinch of salt, Tabasco sauce, and lime juice. Stir guacamole well to mix.
7 Arrange ring of beans on each plate and spoon guacamole into centre.

TO SERVE
Garnish with sprigs of fresh coriander just before serving.

78 TABBOULEH
Serves 6–8

Ingredients
210 g (7 oz) bulghur
1 bunch parsley
2 bunches fresh mint
3 lemons
500 g (1 lb) tomatoes
3 spring onions
125 ml (4 fl oz) olive oil
Cacik
125 g (4 oz) black olives
for serving
6–8 medium pita breads
for serving

TO SERVE
*Serve at room temperature
with a bowl of cacik. Add
olives and sprigs of mint.*

1 Put bulghur in a large bowl and pour over enough cold water to cover generously. Soak for 30 minutes. Drain bulghur thoroughly in sieve or the tabbouleh will be soggy.
2 Strip parsley leaves from stalks and coarsely chop. Do the same with mint leaves.
3 Squeeze juice from lemons; there should be about 125 ml (4 fl oz) juice. Discard any seeds.
4 With tip of small knife, cut round, remove, and discard cores from tomatoes. Cut crosswise in half and squeeze out seeds, then coarsely chop each tomato.
5 Trim and chop spring onions, including some of the green tops.
6 In a large bowl, combine bulghur, tomatoes, spring onions, parsley, lemon juice, olive oil, two-thirds of mint, and plenty of salt and pepper. Mix well. You can add more seasoning, parsley, or mint if required. Cover and chill in refrigerator for at least 2 hours.
7 Prepare cacik (see p.33). Season to taste. Chill in refrigerator for at least 2 hours to allow flavours to blend and mellow.
8 Serve with moist pita breads warmed in oven for 3–5 minutes.

79 MEDITERRANEAN SALAD

Serves 6–8

Ingredients

250 g (8 oz) couscous
1 bunch parsley
2 bunches fresh mint
3 lemons
500 g (1 lb) tomatoes
3 spring onions
125 ml (4 fl oz) olive oil
Tzatziki

1 Put couscous in large bowl and pour over 250 ml (8 fl oz) boiling water, stirring quickly with fork. Leave until plump, about 5 minutes.

2 Empty couscous into a sieve and drain thoroughly, or the salad will be soggy.

3 Coarsley chop parsley and mint leaves.

4 Squeeze juice from lemons; there should be about 125 ml (4 fl oz) juice. Discard any seeds.

5 With tip of small knife, remove and discard cores from tomatoes. Cut crosswise in half and squeeze out seeds; coarsely chop each tomato.

6 Trim and chop spring onions.

7 Make tzatziki (*see p.33*). Chill for at least 2 hours to allow flavours to blend.

8 In a large bowl, combine lemon juice, couscous, tomatoes, spring onions, parsley, olive oil, two-thirds of mint, and plenty of salt and pepper. Mix well. Cover; chill in refrigerator.

TO SERVE
Serve with tzatziki, green olives, pita bread, fresh mint, and lemon slices.

80 PASTA & MUSSEL

Serves 4–6

Ingredients

1 kg (2 lb) mussels
4 shallots
175 ml (6 fl oz) dry
white wine
Pepper
Herb vinaigrette
dressing
250 g (8 oz) fusilli
(pasta spirals)
3 spring onions

1 Prepare and scrub mussels well before cooking (*see p.55*).

2 Peel and chop shallots into fine dice. Put half shallots, wine, and plenty of pepper into large saucepan. Bring to boil; simmer for 2 minutes.

3 Add mussels to saucepan. Cover; cook over high heat for 5–7 minutes until shells open.

4 Transfer mussels to large bowl; leave until cool. Discard any shells that have not opened. Remove mussels from shells.

5 Make herb vinaigrette dressing (*see p.28*) with rest of shallots, parsley, tarragon, lemon juice, and garlic. Season. Pour over mussels; stir well.

6 Add pasta to boiling water; simmer for 8–10 minutes until just tender but still chewy. Drain pasta and add to dressed mussels.

7 Trim spring onions and cut into thin slices. Sprinkle over pasta. Toss salad well and season to taste.

TO SERVE
*Serve with a lemon slice
and tarragon sprig.*

81 HOW TO PREPARE MUSSELS

Mussels should be closed when bought. Discard those that do not close when tapped or that have broken shells. To prepare the mussels for cooking, scrape each shell with a knife to remove any barnacles. Use the back of the knife blade to preserve the sharp edge. Detach and discard any weed or "beard" from each shell. Scrub each shell hard under cold running water. The shells should open when cooked; discard any that remain closed.

82 PASTA & SCALLOP

Serves 4–6

Ingredients

3 garlic cloves; 2 shallots
1 bunch each fresh chives,
tarragon, & parsley
1 lemon
125 ml (4 fl oz) olive oil
45 ml (3 tbsp) cream
500 g (1 lb) scallops
250 g (8 oz) spinach pasta
3 spring onions

1 Dice garlic and shallots. Finely chop chives, tarragon, and parsley.
2 Squeeze juice from lemon. Whisk together lemon juice, shallots, and half garlic only. Gradually whisk in oil so that dressing emulsifies and thickens slightly. Whisk in herbs with double cream. Season.
3 Remove scallops from shells, if necessary discarding crescent-shaped membrane at side. Rinse in cold water and dry. Cut large scallops into 2 rounds.
4 Heat 15 ml (1 tbsp) olive oil in large frying pan. Add scallops with remaining garlic. Season. Sauté until brown and slightly crisp, 1–2 minutes.
5 Cook pasta for 8–10 minutes; slice spring onions. Drain pasta. Toss with spring onions, scallops, and creamy herb dressing.

TO SERVE
Serve at room temperature and garnish each serving with chives.

83 WALDORF CHICKEN SALAD

Serves 6

Ingredients
1 onion; 1 carrot
4 celery sticks, with leaves if possible
1 bouquet garni, made with 5–6 parsley
stalks, 2–3 sprigs fresh thyme, & 1 bay leaf
4 skinless, boneless chicken breasts,
about 750 g (1½ lbs)

1 litre (1¾ pints) water
10–12 black peppercorns
125 g (4 oz) walnut pieces
500 g (1 lb) tart, crisp green apples
1 lemon
175 ml (6 fl oz) bottled mayonnaise
175 ml (6 fl oz) plain yogurt

1 △ Trim and peel onion and carrot; cut into quarters. Trim off tops and leaves of celery. Tie parsley, thyme, and bay into bouquet garni. Strip tendon from underside of each chicken breast.

2 △ Pour water into wide pan. Add peppercorns, celery tops and leaves, onion, carrot, and bouquet garni. Bring to boil; simmer for 10–15 minutes. Add chicken and simmer up to 12 minutes.

3 ◁ Heat oven to 180° C/350° F/gas 4. Bake walnut pieces until crisp, 5–8 minutes. Cut celery into 5 mm (¼ in) slices. Cool chicken in poaching liquid, and pull into 5 cm (2 in) slivers.

4 △ Remove ends from apples, cut in half, and scoop out cores. Cut apples into small cubes. Transfer to large bowl. Cut lemon in half and squeeze juice over apples. Coat well.

5 △ Add chicken, celery, mayonnaise, yogurt, and two-thirds of walnuts to apple. Stir well. Season to taste. Cover; chill in refrigerator for 1 hour. Coarsely chop remaining walnuts for garnish.

TO SERVE
Serve in individual bowls with chopped walnuts sprinkled over the top.

84 TROPICAL CHICKEN
Serves 6

Ingredients
1 onion; 1 carrot
4 celery sticks
Bouquet garni
1 litre (1¾ pints) water
10–12 black peppercorns
4 skinless, boneless chicken
breasts, 750 g (1½ lbs)
1 melon, 500 g (1 lb)
1 papaya, 250 g (8 oz)
1 mango, 375 g (12 oz)
250 ml (8 fl oz) yogurt
1.25 ml (¼ tsp) each
cardamom & coriander
1 lemon

1 Trim and peel onion and carrot; cut into quarters. Trim off tops and leaves of celery. Make bouquet garni of parsley, thyme, and bay.
2 Pour water into wide pan. Add peppercorns, vegetables, and bouquet garni. Bring to boil; simmer for 10–15 minutes.
3 Strip tendon from underside of each chicken breast. Add to pan; simmer up to 12 minutes.
4 Halve melon and papaya. Discard seeds and cut out flesh with melon baller into bowl.
5 Halve mango and cut out cubes of flesh into bowl. Break chicken into slivers; add to bowl.
6 Make dressing with plain yogurt, ground herbs, and lemon juice. Season to taste. Add to bowl, stir well.

TO SERVE
Serve on a large platter garnished with lemon twists and mint sprigs.

85 TERIYAKI CHICKEN
Serves 4

Ingredients

1.25 cm (½ in) root ginger
1 garlic clove
125 ml (4 fl oz) soy sauce
30 ml (2 tbsp) granulated sugar
45 ml (3 tbsp) rice wine
45 ml (3 tbsp) sesame oil
125 ml (4 fl oz) vegetable oil
1 red pepper
4 boneless, skinless chicken breasts, 750 g (1½ lbs)
1 cos lettuce
125 g (4 oz) bean sprouts

1 To make marinade, finely chop ginger and garlic. Add to soy sauce, sugar, 15 ml (1 tbsp) each of rice wine and sesame oil, and 30 ml (2 tbsp) vegetable oil.

2 To make dressing, transfer 60 ml (4 tbsp) of marinade to another bowl, add rest of rice wine and sesame oil. Whisk in rest of vegetable oil. Taste, season, and set aside.

2 Cut pepper into thin strips. Place in dressing and leave to soften, 1–2 hours.

3 Strip tendons from chicken breasts. Place in dish, pour over marinade, cover, and refrigerate for 1–2 hours, turning breasts 3–4 times.

5 Grill chicken breasts, brushing often with marinade until well browned, 5–7 minutes each side. Once cooked, cool. Slice thinly.

6 Shred lettuce into strips. Place bean sprouts in bowl, cover with boiling water and let stand for 1 minute. Drain, rinse, drain again.

7 Put lettuce and bean sprouts in large bowl. Add pepper strips with dressing; toss to mix.

TO SERVE
Arrange sliced chicken on large plates with the salad to one side.

86 WILTED SPINACH SALAD
Serves 6

Ingredients
½ French baguette
45 ml (3 tbsp) olive oil
1 garlic clove
2 eggs
500 g (1 lb) fresh spinach
250 g (8 oz) streaky bacon rashers
75 ml (5 tbsp) red wine vinegar

TO SERVE
Pile salad on individual plates, sprinkle with egg white and yolk, and serve with croûtes.

1 Heat oven to 200° C/400° F/ gas 6. Cut baguette into thin slices, brush with olive oil; bake until toasted, turning slices once, 7–10 minutes.
2 Remove skin from garlic clove, cut in half, and rub on each slice of toasted bread.
3 Hard-boil and shell eggs. Separate yolks from whites: finely dice whites, sieve yolks. Wash and dry spinach leaves; place in bowl.
4 Chop bacon into strips; cook in frying pan until crisp, 3–5 minutes. Add bacon and fat to spinach. Pour vinegar into frying pan, boil for 1 minute. Pour into bowl. Toss salad well.

87 YANKEE POTATO SALAD

Serves 6–8

Ingredients

1.4 kg (3 lb) new potatoes
8 eggs
125 ml (4 fl oz) mayonnaise
60 ml (4 tbsp) soured cream
45 ml (3 tbsp) red
wine vinegar
15 ml (1 tbsp) Dijon
mustard
1 small bunch parsley
1 small bunch radishes
3 celery sticks
2 pickled cucumbers
1 medium onion

TO SERVE
Garnish servings
with wedges of egg
and parsley sprigs.

1 Scrub potatoes under cold, running water. If using large potatoes, cut into smaller pieces. Boil gently until tender, 15–20 minutes. Drain well.

2 Hard boil eggs for 10 minutes. Cut 4 eggs in quarter wedges for garnish; chop others.

3 Stir mayonnaise, cream, vinegar, Dijon mustard, and parsley leaves together. Season.

4 Cut radishes, celery, and cucumbers (or gherkins) into thin slices. Finely dice onion.

5 Transfer potatoes to large bowl. Add other ingredients. Pour dressing over salad, stir to mix. Season.

88 BLACK FOREST POTATO SALAD

Serves 6–8

Ingredients

1.4 kg (3 lb) new potatoes
1 small red onion
45 ml (3 tbsp) red
wine vinegar
45 ml (3 tbsp) soured cream
30 ml (2 tbsp) hot mustard
10 ml (2 tsp) caraway seeds
250 ml (8 fl oz) safflower oil
7–10 sprigs parsley
150 g (5 oz) thin-sliced ham

1 Cook potatoes as above.

2 To make the vinegar and caraway dressing, peel and finely dice onion. Put in bowl with red wine vinegar, soured cream, and hot mustard. Season. Sprinkle in caraway seeds. Whisk together until just mixed; gradually whisk in safflower oil so that dressing emulsifies and thickens. Season to taste. Coarsely chop parsley.

3 Thinly slice potatoes. Transfer to large bowl. Add dressing; mix until thoroughly coated.

4 Cut ham into strips. Mix with parsley in salad.

89 CAESAR SALAD

Serves 6–8

Ingredients

1 large cos lettuce, about
1 kg (2 lb)
6 garlic cloves
6 anchovy fillets
15 ml (1 tbsp) Dijon mustard
Pepper

Juice of 1 lemon
225 ml (8 fl oz) olive oil
1 egg (or 30 ml, 2 tbsp, double cream)
Garlic croutons, made with ½ day-old,
French baguette
125 g (4 oz) freshly grated
Parmesan cheese

TO SERVE
*Serve directly from salad bowl,
passing the remaining cheese
and croutons separately.*

1 △ Discard root of lettuce; tear leaves into small pieces. Peel and finely chop 3 garlic cloves. Drain anchovy fillets, place in large salad bowl, and crush with fork. Add garlic, mustard, and pepper. Pour in lemon juice; stir dressing well. Whisk in 175 ml (6 fl oz) oil. Add lettuce; toss well.

2 △ Crack egg into small bowl; add to salad leaves and dressing. Toss together well. Make croutons (*see right*); add half with most of Parmesan to salad and toss well again. Add salt if required.

90 HOW TO MAKE CROUTONS

Crispy garlic-flavoured croutons are an essential part of Caesar and other salads. Sliced white bread can be used, although a day-old French baguette is preferable.

1 △ Cut half a French baguette into 1.25 cm (½ in) slices. Stack a few slices up and cut into cubes, leaving on crust. Repeat with remaining slices. Peel skin from 3 garlic cloves.

2 △ Heat 60 ml (4 tbsp) olive oil in frying pan. Add garlic cloves and bread. Stir constantly until croutons are golden, 2–3 minutes. Tip croutons onto paper towels to drain. Discard garlic.

1 △ Boil potatoes. Top and tail beans. Boil until tender, 5–7 minutes. Make dressing with vinegar, and chopped thyme and chervil (*see p.28*).

2 △ Hard-boil eggs for 10 minutes. Shell each egg and cut into quarters. Peel tomatoes (*see p.19*) and cut into wedges. Drain both tuna and anchovies.

3 △ Flake tuna in bowl with fork. Stir in 75 ml (5 tbsp) dressing. Arrange potatoes in large serving bowl. Toss beans in 45 ml (3 tbsp) dressing; arrange in centre; spoon tuna on top.

4 △ Alternate a few egg and tomato wedges on top of tuna and place the rest of the wedges around edge of bowl. Briskly whisk remaining dressing and spoon over salad.

92 FRESH TUNA NIÇOISE

Cut 1 kg (2 lb) fresh tuna into cubes; thread on 6 skewers, alternating with tomato wedges. Marinate in herb dressing (*see p.28*) for 1 hour. Season tuna and grill for about 2 minutes. Turn and baste with marinade; grill for 2 minutes more. Prepare salad as above. Place kebabs on top, pour over dressing; serve.

93 PRAWN & COURGETTE
Serves 6

Ingredients
1 pinch saffron threads
30 ml (2 tbsp) hot water
2 lemons
6 garlic cloves
60 ml (4 tbsp) white wine vinegar
250 ml (8 fl oz) olive oil
60 ml (4 tbsp) capers
500 g (1 lb) courgettes
18 unpeeled jumbo prawns

TO SERVE
Pile courgettes in centre of each plate and surround with prawns.

1 Put saffron threads in a medium bowl and pour hot water over them. Leave for 5 minutes.
2 Squeeze juice from lemons. Peel and coarsely chop garlic. Add lemon juice, garlic, vinegar, olive oil, and capers to saffron. Season. Stir well, crushing capers to extract flavour.
3 Trim courgettes; halve and finely slice.
4 Transfer courgettes to shallow dish; add two-thirds of marinade. Toss to coat; cover, and leave in refrigerator to marinate, 3–4 hours.
5 Prepare prawns (*see p.67*). Place in dish, spoon remaining marinade over top, toss to coat; cover, and marinate in refrigerator, 3–4 hours.
6 Place courgettes in frying pan; simmer until tender, 3–5 minutes.
7 Place prawns in grill pan, cut-side-up. Brush with marinade and spoon over capers. Grill for 3–4 minutes until pink and sizzling.

94 PRAWN & MUSHROOM
Serves 6

Ingredients
3 lemons
6 garlic cloves
60 ml (4 tbsp) white wine
vinegar
250 ml (8 fl oz) olive oil
60 ml (4 tbsp) capers
18 unpeeled jumbo prawns
375 g (12 oz) button
mushrooms

1 Squeeze juice from two lemons into bowl. Peel and coarsely chop garlic. Add with vinegar, olive oil, and capers to bowl. Season. Stir well, crushing capers to extract flavour.

2 Prepare prawns (*see below*). Place in dish, spoon one-third marinade over top, toss to coat; cover, and marinate in refrigerator, 3–4 hours.

3 Wipe mushrooms with damp paper towels, then trim stalks up to caps. Bring small pan of salted water to boil. Add mushrooms, simmer, 5–7 minutes. Drain, rinse, drain again.

4 Add mushrooms to remaining marinade; stir, cover, and marinate in refrigerator, 3–4 hours.

5 Place prawns in grill pan, cut-side-up. Brush with marinade and spoon over capers. Grill for 3–4 minutes until pink and sizzling. Serve immediately while still hot.

To Serve
Garnish each serving with a slice of lemon and a sprig of parsley.

95 HOW TO PREPARE JUMBO PRAWNS

Hold each prawn, underside-up, on a chopping board. Leaving the tail intact, cut each prawn in half to open in a butterfly shape. Turn over and pull out and discard the dark intestinal vein running along the back of every one. Rinse each prawn well under cold, running water and transfer to a paper towel to dry.

SALAD KNOW-HOW

96 DECORATING A SALAD

The presentation of a salad can be improved dramatically with an attractive, eye-catching decoration, such as an apple chevron, a citrus coronet, a lemon twist, a salmon rose, or a mint and cherry tomato.

- To make cucumber crescents, cut strips lengthwise from the side of a cucumber with a canelle knife. If the skin has been waxed, peel it completely. Then cut the cucumber in half lengthwise and scoop out the seeds. Cut it into thin, crosswise slices. Fan out the crescents with your hand.

LEMON TWISTS
To make a lemon twist, thinly slice a lemon. Remove the pips. Cut each slice along the radius; open and twist on the cut.

97 GARNISHING A SALAD

The best salad garnishes are those which feature in the flavours of the salad itself. Fresh herbs, pared vegetable peel, blanched citrus zest, hard-boiled egg, strips of toasted tortilla, tomato or radish roses, fresh berries, and toasted nuts are all attractive and tasty. For contrast, add fried croutons, or grated or shaved Parmesan cheese.

FLOWER GARNISHES

98 USING SALAD SERVERS

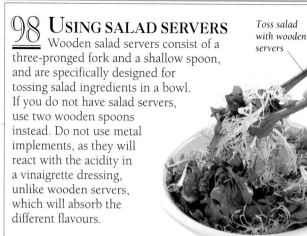

Toss salad with wooden servers

Wooden salad servers consist of a three-pronged fork and a shallow spoon, and are specifically designed for tossing salad ingredients in a bowl. If you do not have salad servers, use two wooden spoons instead. Do not use metal implements, as they will react with the acidity in a vinaigrette dressing, unlike wooden servers, which will absorb the different flavours.

99 USING A WOODEN BOWL

You can use almost any bowl for tossing salad, provided it is not made of aluminium or enamel, which, like cutlery, will react with the acid in vinaigrette. A wooden bowl is best, as it becomes impregnated with the dressing and soon acquires a flavour of its own.

100 ONE BOWL OR MANY?

Most salads can be served in one large bowl, but some, known as "composed" salads, should be served as separate ingredients on individual plates for a more attractive presentation.

STACK OF
SALAD
BOWLS

101 STORING SALADS

Most salad ingredients can be prepared ahead and stored. Lettuce and other salad greens can be trimmed, washed, and kept in a refrigerator for up to a day, loosely wrapped in a damp tea towel. Do not dress greens until you are ready to serve them, as the acidic element of the dressing will wilt the leaves. Root vegetables, such as carrots and potatoes, are more robust, and can be prepared and dressed a few hours before serving.

INDEX

91 SALAD NIÇOISE
Serves 6

Ingredients

1 kg (2 lb) potatoes
375 g (12 oz) French beans
Herb vinaigrette dressing
125 ml (4 fl oz) red wine vinegar
7-10 sprigs fresh thyme

1 bunch fresh chervil
6 eggs
500 g (1 lb) medium tomatoes
2 x 200 g (7 oz) cans tuna
10 anchovy fillets
125 g (4 oz) black olives

TO SERVE
*Arrange olives and
crosses of anchovy fillets
inside the egg and tomato border.*